The Moon & All Her Stars

Ky Dale

BookLeaf Publishing

Presentation by *BookLeaf Publishing*

Web: www.bookleafpub.com

E-mail: info@bookleafpub.com

ISBN: 9789357613248

First edition 2022

DEDICATION

A.M.D. I did it, I hope you can see it up there.

ACKNOWLEDGEMENT

I would like to thank my grandmother for pushing me to keep chasing my love for writing & supporting me through everything I did. You are the strongest woman I know and I pray to god that I make you proud with what I do.

I would like to thank my found family. They have been the most supportive group of people I have ever met. When the going got tough they were right there with me, I was never alone again. This book wouldn't have been possible without them. Thank you for giving me the opportunity to make something beautiful, it really wouldn't be here without you guys.

Lastly, I would like to thank Book Leaf Publishing! I can be as sentimental as I want but this book literally would not be in its most tangible form without these guys. Thank you for giving so many aspiring authors like myself the chance to put ourselves out there.

PREFACE

To The Reader-
All my life I have been writing things down and trying to turn them into something beautiful. At first, it was a distraction from the harsh realities of life and now, it's my passion. These poems are about real people, real experiences, and real memories. For that reason, when I started writing I didn't think I would ever let my work see the light of day but, here we are. This started as a hobby, I would have never imagined that I would be publishing my writing and it's still so hard to believe. So many people told me that this was an unrealistic goal, but I want to tell you that it's not. If there is even an ounce of your soul that wants to follow that "unrealistic" or "unattainable" dream, follow it. I am over the moon to have gotten the chance to share these pieces, thank you!

The Sun & The Moon

When the sun loves the moon nobody wins
except those who witness their exchange
The sun will desperately follow the moon
wishing that light years were minutes
The moon will patiently await the equinoxes
when she gets to see her lover the longest
The sun will dread those equal days until he
explodes.
The sun and the moon love each other dearly
though
They exchange beautiful moments
They create the things scientists will gawk over
for decades
They make the most wonderful memories
But that is all they will ever have, memories and
moments, beautiful phenomenons
They just aren't meant for each other
The moon loves the tides the sun sets over
And she knows he was here first
She knows it should be him that she gazes at
It should be him that she desperately pulls in
But it’s just not in the cards for them.
The sun knows that the moon will never not love
her tides
He knows that they are meant to be together

They are light years apart and yet she pulls the
tides effortlessly
They will gravitate to her & she will embrace
them even if they exist on different planes
It's a science, He knows this.
So he will accept her phases and dread the
painful equinoxes all the same
He will love her from afar
They will continue to make spectacular
phenomenons and he will cherish their eclipses
He will not explode, there will be no grand
conclusion
The Moon loves The Tides
The Sun loves The Moon
And that's okay
They will always have the memories

Dream Girl

You and I both know that I am not your dream
girl
I'd be willing to bet I'm not even the girl you'd
settle for
I've said it from the start of whatever this was
I know exactly what I am to you
I am the girl you use as masturbation material
when the night gets too lonely
I am the girl you scoff at when you see whatever
skanky outfit I put on this morning
You crack misogynistic jokes about the way I act
with your buddies behind closed doors
I have grown to accept the fact that we are oil
and water
we will never mix, we will never be compatible
in the way that a dog needs his leash.
we will forever only make each other worse
in the same way that pouring water on an oil fire
will only make it spread
only heighten the threat, you need salt.
you are the kind of boy that needs to be stopped
before he spreads
you collect watery girls like there is a national
drought

each one making you more dangerous, more
aggressive than the last
I pray one day you find an ocean
the way she moves and masquerades as the
water you so desperately need
only to rip you away from the shore
and suffocate your fire with her salt.

Small

I miss being small.
I miss how tiny I used to look next to my older cousins.
I miss the childlike excitement that kept me up all night before the first day of school.
I miss getting stuffed animals for Christmas.
I miss being able to walk into my bedroom and find clothes that were laid out for me.
I miss being able to go shopping with my mom finding cute back-to-school clothes that fit into dress code.
I miss being looked at as smart and talented.
I miss being looked at as a friend.
I miss friendships that didn't have strings.
I miss being someone's friend rather than their late-night fantasy.
I don't care that you want to fuck me in my office.
I don't care that you want to fuck me on my bike.
I don't care that you want to fuck me in the back of your car.
I don't fucking care.
What happened to friends?
Were we ever friends?

or is this another one of those games where
we're friends until you confess
and then I'm supposed to oblige no matter how
bad it makes my skin crawl
because I'm a good friend.
I'm the friend that kisses your wounds and
patches you up and gives you advice
so of course!
why wouldn't I do this too?
why wouldn't I be everything you've ever
touched yourself to?
I'm the hot girl with daddy issues after all!
I'm the girl who can't say no after all!
It's been drilled into my head that my voice
saying no
is followed by a smack and a sting that doesn't
go away after all!
I'm scrubbing my skin red to get you off of me
after all!
This isn't the first boiling hot shower I've taken
to melt someone's touch off me after all!
I should have expected this after all!
I'm just a game to you after all!
Nobody wants to love the psycho
so why should I expect different?
I'm kinky and freaky and hot and I dress like a
whore,
I've got just enough daddy issues to make it the
best sex of your life

and enough mommy issues to make sure you get
exactly what you want.
I will make you feel everything I've been feeling
all my life
and for a few days,
or a few hours,
or let's be honest here,
a few minutes
it's freeing and it's new and it's exciting.
But then it's overwhelming
and scary
and way way too much for you to handle
so you leave.
no one wants to love the psycho.
no one wants to be anything close to committed
with the whore.
You just want to be friends
until you want to fuck.

Exit Here

I can now wholeheartedly say that I don't care
when you threaten to kill yourself
It feels as common as taking my medication in
the morning
Just another part of the mundane daily routine I
fell into
Wake up in a room that's too hot and too cold at
the same time
Never comfortable in my own bed
Shower only to rub my skin raw trying to wash
last night off of me
The everlasting feeling that I will never be clean
of you
Brush yellow teeth that I hardly care for
anymore
Most of them are fake now anyway
Money can't buy happiness but it can buy
appearances
Take meds that you forced me to need
The codependency I had for you wasn't enough
You needed me to be reliant on a disease so I
would behave
Be weak to your will
Fight like we do every day when I do the latest
idiotic thing that pisses you off

At some point, I got tired of being your
punching bag
At some point, I started fighting back
Try to leave because its one of the few tactics
I've found resolves our issues
Not the leaving but the trying
Not actually forcing you into my absence but
making you remember that I could
Forcing you to recognize that I don't need you
anymore
"I swear to god if you walk out that door I'll put
a bullet in my brain"
And leaving
Letting the door slam behind me because I know
that you won't kill yourself over me
You wouldn't hurt your precious appearances
over the girl you cheat on
You could never admit that the threats are as
empty as the gun you swing around
You know you lost
You know that I have the power now
And it's not that I gained anything
It's that I lost the will to keep you alive
I lost the ache in my heart when you started to
cry
I forgot what it felt like to love you
What it feels like to view you as a partner and
not an enemy

To see you as more than a menial task I have to put up with
So now when I get the texts even all these years later
I leave them on delivered
I put my phone on do not disturb
I sleep well knowing that if you were going to kill yourself
You would have done it when I left you for the last time
The last time was years ago
And here you are
Still breathing
Still walking around
Like you didn't try to make me your savior

"God"

You are what brought me back to faith
And it wasn’t a sermon that convinced me
There was no holy book to pour myself into
There was no preacher in front of the pews
There were no hymns or homilies
There was no legend or myth
It was the way your hand cupped the small of my back
It was the way you ran calloused fingers over my cheekbone
It was the way your voice glided in the air
How it pooled like warm wax in the coldest parts of me
It was how your eyes lingered on my skin
How it almost seemed painful for you to look away
I am devoted to you
And maybe it's ghoulish but even today
I love the glint of pain in your eyes when you look away
Because it means you are devoted to me too
You want to stare at me for hours and never look away
I want your gaze to burn holes in my skin as a permanent reminder

I want your touch to stain my skin so I'm never without you
I want to wear you on my neck like a cross
A public declaration that I belong to you
That you are my faith, my religion
I never believed in a higher power
But in finding you I found grace too
I found the reason I wake up in the morning
I figured out what people mean when they say "Keep faith"
I have found my higher power
I have a connection with you that no other believer has
Because I get to stand next to my faith
I am blessed with their presence every day
And they get to have me in a way no other higher being does
They get to hold me and love me close
They are not banished to another realm
To so many, religion is cruel like that
But not to me
Not to us

Corpse

There was no autopsy when I died
No funeral to mourn at
No celebration of all I had accomplished
Because up until recently
Not even I knew I had died, A version of me at least
So when I did realize that I had died
I opened an investigation, I performed my own autopsy
I took the cold shriveled body that was once mine out of her shallow grave
And I cut her open, searching for her cause of death
I collected DNA, I recounted her last known sightings
There were no signs of forced entry
As it turns out, she was friends with her killer
He would tell her the sweetest empty promises
Hold her in the darkest part of the night
Let her cry to him when she couldn't hold it in any longer
And then he finally shot her, right there in her chest
He even handed me the smoking gun when I called him out

So I went back to the coroners' office and collected her remains
I gave myself a proper burial with flowers and all
I lowered my own casket, I held my own hand when I missed her at night
I was my own savior
You don’t get to mourn her
You don’t get to mourn a version of myself I created for you
You get to live with the fact that you killed an innocent girl
When all she wanted to do was love you
You don’t get to be sorry when you're the one who killed me

Cannibal

When you ask me why I love you there is not an
acceptable arrangement of words
There is no sane way to describe my love for
you
So I tell you that I don't know and that we don't
choose
I tell you that I fell in love with the way you
love me
Because I know the familiar face of fear that
comes with my love all too well
I know the look of horror covered by awkward
smiles
The nervous chuckle and anxious collection of
belongings before
"I should really head out, it's getting late. We'll
do this again, soon!"
As if they are trying to convince me that my
love doesn't scare them
That it doesn't repulse them
With you, I pray that I will not kill your love
with mine
So I lie when you ask me why I love you
I can never tell you that I want to open your
skull

Drink from your brain so I may think in the gentle ways you do
That I want to open your chest and eat your heart
So I may love as passionately as you
That I want to crawl inside your skin so that I may move like you
And never be without you again
I can not tell you that I want your blood to paint my walls
Because it is the only hue that could ever possibly encapsulate you
I can not say that I want your teeth to line my neck
So I am never without your smile
I can not say that I want your eyes to sit in a jar on my desk
So I can gaze into them even when you are no longer here
Because if I do
I know that you will run from me
I know that your love for me will die
So I will tell you that I love your eyes and that your smile is kind
I will tell you that your heart is gold and your brain works beautifully
I will keep my true love for you to myself
So that it will not take you away from me too

Till Death

Up, Down, Up

A silver tower looms over me as I stand next to the billet. Green and red peaks exchange motions as they dance across a silver screen, fixed in a blue box. Hooks spring from the tower's peak, pools hang from overhead. A line connects her to the spring, like an anchor on a once brazen vessel. She grips my hand until her small knuckles turn white, she is afraid. And then, she is carried off with the Autumn breeze.

Down, Up, Down

There is a buzz and then a breath. The illness has overtaken her whole. For years she has clawed and scratched her way to wellness. I can no longer blame her for refusing to fight a sickness that has taken her hostage. She has fought and now she will rest. There is a buzz and then, she is lifted out into the sea of stars.

Up, Down, Up

The lights illuminate the world in a mirage of blue and red. Blue complimenting the red stains on the road beneath our feet. I have never been so sad to see purple pools. The sawbones never had a chance to try. The lights carried her into the night so she may never be touched by the day.

Down, Up, Down

She filled the holes in her heart with sugar and snow. The sweetness clogged her nose and clouded her eyes. My own journey awaits me. I trust that her cavities have been filled and her sweet tooth has been mended. Before my journey can begin, hers has come to an abrupt halt. Once more, she is carried away into the autumn breeze. I return to the billet. It was foolish to have left.

Up, Down, Up

Unsteady and fragile as a spring doe.
With each collapse, her strength declines. She is mended and patched with donations and transfusions. Spare parts can not mend what she suffers from. even if it were feasible, spare parts only last so long. So I will stay here at the billet to guide her into the autumn air as I have done

so many times before. I will walk with her to the gates and when they open with angelic choirs and golden rays of light I will let her go. so I may return and guide another into holy hands.

Kill Him

Look at me with scarlet eyes tie your tongue and then,
Cut it off with all your lies because in the end
You told me that you loved me you thought I was "the one"
Drifting eyes caught a glimpse of a girl who knew how to have more fun
You built a web of lies that you eventually got caught in.
I found you out, you cried about, all the things I said
Midnight phone calls and I'm still up wishing you were dead

Unholy

The church stood there, abandoned and decaying
There are bricks missing from her exterior
The doors are locked when he finds her
A lone saint who found such beauty in the ivy vines growing up her walls
He does not mind her imperfections
He would stare at the cracks in her foundation for hours
Running holy hands over her brick walls, the Chapel doesn’t matter to him
When he could love her exterior for ages
The stories that she tells him are sweet in his ears
He will listen to them for hours in the freezing cold
If only to get a glimpse at the architects' vision
Even though he can not enter her halls he always returns
After years of studying her beauty
Memorizing every scratch and scar
After writing a new holy book entirely dedicated to her
Dedicated to the stories she's told him
And the love they have built that fills her cracks
He comes to her, and her doors are open

He runs a warm hand along her, as if to ask
permission to explore her
She settles, relaxing her barriers to him
But not so much that she is free to him
The air is tense, she is so stiff with him at her
entrance
So afraid of being vandalized again
Terrified of her bricks being torn from her walls
like they were so long ago
He breathes into her archway, gently stepping
through the door
And when he enters, It is warm and soft
Her draft falling down his neck
She is as beautiful to him inside as she is out
As he walks through her halls her floors whine
and moan with each step
Deeper, and deeper into this abandoned beauty
He speaks out to the church with every inch he
moves
She knows she is safe with him among her halls
She relaxes, adjusting to his presence within her
And when he lets go to his knees and melts into
her
She forgets the heresy that tainted her
She wonders how she could have kept him
locked out for so long
When his worship feels this good

Betrayal

All it took was one night
Over coffee at 8 pm in your car
I can't remember where you took me
Because your words cloud the memory
All it took was one word
And I played along in search of safety
They say there are three panic responses
Fight, Flight, and Freeze
But I believe there is another,
Facade.

Slasher

You can always tell who's going to die first in a horror film
They're usually too trusting with a splash of childlike naivety.
They sleep with the doors unlocked and the windows open
They practically invite the mask-wearing killer into their home
And we're all supposed to act surprised as they're gutted on camera
No one acts surprised like that in real life
No one will be shocked when this ends poorly
When we break up people will not give you the same fake sympathy they dish out for the ditsy blond actress
They will ask you what you expected knowing me
They will tell you they told you so and laugh when you cry about it
They will not feel bad, you're the one who left your doors unlocked
So when I tell to that I am the killer of all the love in my life
When I tell you the mask I wear is not who I am

That I am much worse than I will ever let you see
When I tell you that you're better off locking those doors and sealing your windows
Believe me, I have been the killer before
Do not let your blood coat my hands too

The Beauty of The Garden

Twenty years ago you were only a seed
He planted you carelessly in damp soil
He had no intention of caring for the bud you would grow into
He planted you by mistake while gazing at the earth's beauty
And when it came time to water the seedling you had become
He had no interest in being a gardener
Miraculously the earth he planted you in allowed your continued growth
And soon you were the most glorious rose
You searched for years for a gardener to care for you
You yearned for the love you were never extended the luxury of
All you found were florists
They cut the wilted flowers off their bush because they were not as pleasing as you
But when they pulled you from the earth they expected you to stay in full bloom
They would rather marvel at your temporary beauty than take care of you
Darling, you have no need for florists or gardeners

You dear, you will do just fine with the rain and sun

Just For You

She is prettier after she cries
Like how the sun seems softer after a storm
She knows the lightning will hurt
But she will give you the most glorious sunset
when she is done

Rose Colored Glasses

There were things she elected to ignore in this arrangement
Assuming they were niche experiences
She would be isolated had she not ignored them
She sought safety in her silence
The rose filter swallowed her oppressors whole
And to her, this unspoken agreement with herself was just life
Until someone unlocked the muzzle
So carefully placed on her by those who feared her tongue
Until a nuclear bomb was dropped on her life
She found peace in the rubble she was left in
The rose filter had shattered
And now, she was going to scream
Until someone finally listened.

Retribution

There is always a moment of hesitation
Right before I release the bomb
My fingers dance above the red button
As if the universe is asking me if I'm sure
And I am always certain
I am exactly what the rumors say
It's their fault for not listening

Coffee at 9pm

I am a time traveler
And I have no control over it
Whispers from new lovers send me to November
Back to his stale breath and empty threats
Back to his car, staring at the cross hanging from his mirror
Praying to a god to let this man take me home
Praying I'm not the next dumb girl in the headlines
Hands in my hair send me to June
When he ripped my head back while we drove
Back to unsolicited comments on my body
And collecting the hair that had fallen out of my head
The smell of beer takes me back years
He smashed a beer bottle over my head
He doesn't remember why he did it
He'll always blame the alcohol
But in those moments I always remember why
At first, I blamed myself for living in the past
Now I blame them for being the reason I do

The Ark

One day you won't need someone to love you anymore
The wanting will never waiver
But there will be a day when their presence is not a necessity
When you can breathe easily without them
There will be a day when all you need is yourself
And that is quite possibly the most freeing part

The Future

I wanted to be in love with you
But nothing seemed to work out
So now our love is poisoned
Words leaving sour tastes in our mouths
This may be it for now
But I will see you when forever ends
Because some people are only meant to sleep
together
Six feet underground

The Hotel

The memories you left with me were cold and brittle
But worst of all they were stuck
like dried pop crusted to cold tile
Every time I thought I'd forgotten, I would step in the sticky mess
And recoil prying my souls from the puddle
But the spot never seemed to come clean
I would mop for hours trying desperately to erase the past
To escape your voice, your words, your touch
But nothing seemed to work
One day I got so sick of hearing my shoe rip from the floor
I sat on my hands and knees with a bucket of bleach
And scrubbed the spot for hours if not days
The stain never fully came off the once white tile
I could point out the reddish brown ring to this day
But at least that fucking sound is gone
At least I don't get stuck on the thought of what you did to me anymore

Now the only person that has to live in those memories
Is you

Rebirth

As everyone eventually finds out, my name isn't actually Ky. My birth name is three letters and 15 years too long. So I changed it in high school and those three letters and 15 years faded into the background. When they find out I'm always asked why I changed it but I never seem to have an answer palatable enough.

My birth name smells like soggy cigarettes and bleach water that has sat unattended for days if not weeks. It tastes like the soapy water that falls into your mouth in the shower, it's not the end of the world when it happens but it's uncomfortable. It looks like the shade of hotel beige my childhood bedroom was painted. Those walls caked with sought from the candles I would burn to fall asleep at night not hopping but, not minding. It sounds like roll call in group therapy and feels like my nails creating the crescent scars in my palms for the first, second, and 50th time.

I always wondered why no one else cringed at the sound of their name. why no one dreaded having substitute teachers and having to explain in front of 30 of your most judgmental peers that "Actually, I don't go by that anymore". When I think of the name I was given before I was given anything else in life I don't even recognize the girl it belonged to. She only wore hoodies and leggings and kept her bleach-fried hair in messy buns. She did everything she could to hide the shape of her body, embarrassed by what she had done to it. She lived in an 8' by 7' room for 2 years so terrified of the rest of the hoarder's house she lived in.

Then I figured out that I didn't have to be so uncomfortable all the time. I didn't have to dread roll call, or substitutes. I could take the rock out of my shoe and walk normally for the first time in my life. So I carved those three stupid letters off of me for a full year before they finally fell to the ground, shattering into millions of pieces. And sometimes someone will step on a shard of my old name but it's nothing that tweezers and a bandaid can't fix. It's nothing like the sickening gashes that name gave me for so many years.

My new name, my real name, smells like eucalyptus and spearmint. It tastes like the lemon scones my partner bakes for me on my birthday. It looks like cliffs of cosmic dust and feels like waking up in a warm bed. My name is the biggest reminder that I don't have to stay in that 8' by 7' room. That I can move out of the hoarder's house. That I can get up and scrub the sought off the walls and paint them white. That I decide how I will live the rest of my life for however long I want.

I don't sleep with the candles lit anymore. I blew them out for the last time 4 years ago, nightlights are safer anyway.

9 789357 613248

Printed by Libri Plureos GmbH in Hamburg, Germany